The Healing Station

Acknowledgements
Thanks to the editors of the following, in which some of these poems first appeared: *Frogmore Papers*, *Orbis*, *London Grip*, *Queen's Quarterly*, *The North*.

Also by Michael McCarthy
Birds' Nests and Other Poems (Bradshaw books)
At the Races (smith|doorstop books)
The Story of Noah and the Ark (Barefoot Books)
The Story of Daniel and the Lion's Den (Barefoot Books)

Grateful thanks to artist Wendy Dison for permission to use her painting Ventana on the front cover. www.wendydison.com

The Healing Station
Michael McCarthy

smith|doorstop

Published 2015 by
smith|doorstop Books
The Poetry Business
Bank Street Arts
32-40 Bank Street
Sheffield S1 2DS
www.poetrybusiness.co.uk

ISBN 978-1-910367-34-6

British Library Cataloguing-in-Publication Data.
A catalogue record for this book is available from the
British Library.

Typeset by Utter
Printed by Ingram/Lightning Source
Cover image: Ventana by Wendy Dison
Author photo: Michelle Neville

smith|doorstop is a member of Inpress,
www.inpressbooks.co.uk. Distributed by Central Books Ltd.,
99 Wallis Road, London E9 5LN.

The Poetry Business is an Arts Council
National Portfolio Organisation

Supported by
ARTS COUNCIL
ENGLAND

Contents

Introductory Note

The National Centre for Arts and Health based at the Adelaide & Meath Hospital in Dublin seeks, among other things, to explore the therapeutic benefit of the arts in health care. This includes exhibitions, live performances, creative writing classes, arts therapies, design projects and participatory art sessions on wards and in waiting rooms, as well as presentations on its work in both medical and arts settings. It also commissions artists in residence as part of a wider project to create a narrative of common illnesses in the arts.

Susan Sontag wrote of illness as a form of citizenship most of us will attain during our lifetime. Age-related illnesses such as stroke and dementia offer a most challenging citizenship. The suddenness of a stroke often means an unexpected and fundamental change in function, communication, and body image which challenges our vulnerability, our physical and cognitive self-image, and our relationship to others and the environment. Dementia with its inherent loss of orientation, working memory, and language skills, is usually the result of Alzheimers and stroke disease and is now one of the biggest challenges facing us as a society. Those who treat and care for patients with stroke and dementia are also directly challenged in engaging with this new citizenship.

Giving a voice to the experience of patient and carer through poetic narrative allows a deeper understanding of this journey with its milestones of despair, challenge, acceptance, recovery, hope and humour. It may also help to create a broader understanding of the changes needed in our approach to age-related illnesses as a wider community with a growing citizenship of older adults, often disenfranchised by a hyper-cognitive world that has not harnessed technological advances fully to allow greater inclusion.

As part of an Irish Arts Council-funded project to create a narrative of stroke in contemporary Irish arts and literature, Michael McCarthy was commissioned as writer in residence in 2012. Over a three month period he facilitated creative writing classes giving staff and patients an opportunity to explore their creativity. He also observed and interacted with staff and patients, and in particular those affected by stroke and dementia. The poems in this collection were written in response to that experience.

– Dr Rónán Collins

My thanks to Dr Rónán Collins for inviting me to do the residency, to The National Centre for Arts and Health for sponsoring it and to the Meath Foundation for financial support. These poems are dedicated to the patients and staff at the Adelaide and Meath Hospital, Tallaght, Dublin.

FAST

Face: A flat tire on one side
        Her smile is Coco the clown

Arms: Can't remember what they're for
        Can't raise them in surrender

Speech: Words wobbling like a drunken butterfly
        Refuse to get in a straight line

Time: Don't waste any
        Call 999 NOW

Taking it all in

You get there early that first warm September morning.
You sit outside, in the courtyard by the day hospital.

You see a large leathery snail making his way
Across the square stone tiles. At full stretch now

And with his horns extended, he sniffs a left turn
And his whole body goes into a graceful curve

Like a tram in slow motion rounding a corner.
Overhead, on the slanted roof a black crow

Grips in his beak a lump of white bread.
Close by, in the laurels behind the twin seat

In memory of Dorothy and David Mitchell,
Physicians, Adelaide Hospital.1909-1995.

A blackbird waits, taking it all in.

Summer of Love

He was frying a few rashers
when the plate fell out of his hand.
I heard the crash coming from the kitchen.
I found him on the floor, his eyes as big as saucers
staring at the ceiling. I kept asking him what happened
but he didn't answer me, his eyes just kept getting bigger.

I rang our son and he called the ambulance.
They put him on the stretcher. I could see
he didn't want them strapping him in,
he's always hated confined spaces.
I sat next to him in the ambulance.
They went straight up to theatre.

I got an asthma attack waiting in the day room
I was convinced he wouldn't come out of it.
When they brought him down here to the ward
he was heavily sedated. I held onto his hand all night
in case he went on me. His voice came back to him
this afternoon, but he's still not right in his head.

'We thought you wouldn't make it,' I told him.
'You'll never know how grateful we all are.'
And would you believe what he said to me!
'You'll never know how grateful I'm not.'
He can't bear the thought. He'd give up
on me if he was given half a chance.

I don't know what'll happen, how long he'll be in here.
They can't tell me anything, they don't know themselves.
The house is only small. There's not near enough room
for a bed downstairs, and I'm not able to lift him.

We met in 67. Summer of love they called it.
We were married forty one years this May.
We haven't spent a night apart since.
I'll not be able to sleep at home tonight.

Bungee Jump

'We're going to lift you onto the hoist, Tony,
then we'll move you over to the physio department.'
He sits back into the leather harness, his legs dangling.
He looks around and then down, studying the distance
as if he's getting himself ready to take the plunge.
But he's had his Bungee jump. He went all the way
to the bottom and didn't bounce.

Lowering him onto the plinth she says: 'try to
sit square to me,' because he's listing badly,
'I'm in the middle, can you match yourself to me?'
She rotates his left arm both ways, then strokes
the back of his hand with a quill. 'Can you feel that?
Now see if you can do it.' He strokes the back of
his bad hand with the quill. 'Watch yourself do it.

Now give me the quill. Now take it off me again.
Ok, sit back. Try to relax this leg. Can you move it?
Look at it, watch it move. Now move your right leg
towards me? Lift it onto my knee. Come on Tony,
push me away with your foot. Do that again.
Stamp your foot on the ground. Again. Good.'

She massages his bad leg with his good hand, then
gets him to do it, gets him to massage his bad hand
with his good one. 'Bring your hand to my shoulder?
Now the other. Look at me. Push me away, try
to get rid of me. Easy now, no need to head butt!
Well done. Rest them on your lap. And relax.'

Hippy Hippy Shake

Arriving at the plinth Tony does the usual warm-ups. He knows them
by heart but it doesn't get easier. Some days it feels like he's back
to square one. Steve helps him to the parallel bars, a five yard stretch
where he can support himself on both sides. He walks slowly forward

and back, then sideways leading with his good leg, he can't do it
with the other leg yet. Maura watches from the side-line, so she can
help him when he comes home. They've moved the bed down-stairs.
They've installed a walk-in shower in what was the broom cupboard.

Now Liz takes over. Standing next to him with her arm round his waist
she sways gently, right to left, left to right. 'Loosen up the hinges a bit.'
Then, she shunts him sideways with her hip, gets him to do the same.
'Come on Tony, let's rock, gimme the hip. Again. And again. Good.'

Maura knows that glint in his eye. There's life in the old devil yet.
The Hippy Hippy Shake by *The Swinging Blue Jeans*, doing it
to Dickie Rock's cover at the dance hall in Tallaght circa 1971.
Now she'd settle for a waltz: *Dublin in the Rare Ould Times*.

Later, she wheels him outside to the courtyard for a smoke.
He knows it's not good for him but he can't give them up.
A smile flickers between them. 'Gimme the hip,' he says.
She laughs. 'You'll have to wait 'til I get you home.'

No Smoke Without Smoke

When she draws on it a bright red glow lights up
like brakes coming on at night. 'My daughter
got it for me off the internet. It's very satisfying.
They don't allow you smoke the real ones in here.'

'Good morning Doctor,' she says, taking a good pull.
'Good morning Molly, and how are you feeling today?'
'Grand altogether Doctor,' she says, taking another pull.
'Did you think about what I said to you yesterday?'

'It's not on Doctor,' she says, shaking her head.
'Why is that Molly?' 'Because it's not to my liking.
I've always looked after myself, always minded
my own business, if you know what I mean.'

But he hasn't backed off. 'I know you're doing
well, but you're not ready to be on your own yet.'
She's pulling at it full throttle now, and thinking:
'there was a time I'd have this fella for breakfast.'

She's searching for a knockout punch. You can see
its slow arrival light up her eyes and spread right across
her face as far as her ears. She takes a long relaxed pull
and settles into her chair. 'In any case, you're not my doctor.'

The Travellers

I got to the halting site, over next to the Red Cow
before the traffic got heavy. I prepared the veggies,
put on the dinner, cleaned and tidied up the caravan.
Then we settled around the table for the home-work.
The boys were good with figures, adding up, anything
to do with making money. Genevieve preferred stories
and poems. When I read her *The Stolen Child* she was
enchanted. You could hear her whispering it: *Come away,*
O human child, – she was convinced it was about herself –
To the waters and the wild, until she had it off by heart.

I'd just popped in to the kitchen to check the spuds, when
all of a sudden my legs started trying to trip each other up.
I held on to the worktop to steady myself, then managed to
zig zag to the couch and throw myself onto it. Genevieve
God help her she's only nine, sat next to me chatting away
as if nothing had happened. I tried to talk back to her but
I couldn't. The words were after going thick in my mouth.
Every now and then she'd smile, and ask if I was alright
or if I wanted a drink of water. The lads carried on with
the sums keeping their heads down as if they didn't notice.

In the end Genevieve ran across to her uncle's caravan.
I could hear her telling him: 'Auntie Josie is very drunk.'
She knew what drunk was from seeing her poor mother
God rest her. Everybody at the site knew I didn't drink.
He came running across the yard to see what was wrong.
The next thing, they were putting me in the ambulance.
The next thing after that I woke up here. Six weeks now
and I'm doing a lot better. I know where things are but
I can't find them. My brain isn't telling the rest of me
what to do. I want to go back if I can get myself right.

Yellow Pages

First, she drums her fingers on the table as if
dancing a slow jig, or loosening up for piano practise.
Then he brings her the telephone. 'Pick up the receiver.'
She struggles, contorting her body to get at an angle.
'Raise your elbow, now dial your home number.'
'I never dial with that hand,' she says.
'I like to listen with my other ear.'

He takes down the Yellow Pages. 'Have a look in there
for a carpenter.' She pages through to C.
'Plenty carpenters in here,' she says.
'Good. Now, see if you can find me a Garden Centre.
I need some shrubs for my patio.' She flips forward,
goes too far, fumbles back, until she finds it.
'Would you mind dialling one of them for me?

Take a look under Travel Agent. I could do with
a holiday.' When she gets to Thomas Cook he asks her
to dial it. Next he calls out: 'Tree Surgeon. I need one of those,
I've got this tree by the garage that's getting out of hand.'
When she finds Washing Machine she's ready
to give it a rest. 'That's very good,' he says.
'Now let's try it all again from the back.'

This time she starts with Yoga. 'I'm sure you've tried that.
Do you need any Tyres? Have you any use for Scrap Metal?
How about Pest Control? You can have Musical Instruments
or Motorbike Repair. Ladders, let's keep away from ladders.
Funeral Directors, ditto. Chiropodist, Acupuncture.'
When she gets as far as Abattoir she's tired.
Yellow Pages goes back on the shelf.

White Board

As he helps her to the White Board, she carries a slight drag
on her right leg. She takes a blue felt pen
in her left hand and begins to draw.
An owl, a pair of ducks, a fox sliding
through a hole in the hedge. When she
swaps to her right it's a different matter.

She stands sideways to the board and begins to doodle.
Chinese characters, or misshapen African butterflies,
or a troupe of tiny figurines, only they lack coherence.
She draws a circle, craggy at the edges. When it gets
to where it started the ends don't meet.

She rubs everything out and begins again. This time
the circle is shaky but passable. Taking a red pen
she adds a pair of eyes, has a go at a smiley mouth.
It's lopsided, and not where it's supposed to be.
'Self Portrait,' she says: 'Me when
I was having the stroke.'

This is the point where she drops the pen. She can't
stoop that far. As she struggles to retrieve it he watches
but doesn't move. After four futile attempts, and close
to exhaustion she succeeds. 'Well done,' he says.
'See how far you've come.'

I'm in Bed

Watching telly. It's around eleven. I feel a sudden
pressure on my jaw. I put my hand to my face to fix it. It keeps
tightening something fierce and the feeling begins to ebb
from my arm. I'm in such a panic I'm afraid I'll pass out.

The next thing I'm spitting and drooling. I can think
of the words but they're coming out back to front.
I try to wake Tom, he's used to me making
odd noises, but by some miracle I manage.

He drags me across the bed. I can see him running
his fingers along the soles of my feet, but I only feel it
on one of them. I think, O Jesus my leg is gone as well.
I keep pinching myself for a response but there is none.

It lasts about ten minutes. Then slowly my leg begins
to come back to me. I'm only thirty seven. We've two children,
Miriam the youngest is two and a half, there's not a bother on her.

Rosalin is four, she wouldn't come and talk to me on the phone.
I had to insist. In the end she came. She was all casual like
as if she was busy with something else.

Craniectomy

The word 'critical' has brought them from the four directions.
He is already in theatre by the time the first of them arrive.
Through the three hour marathon they wait, hoping against hope.

When the surgeon walks in they can hardly breathe.
The operation has gone better than they feared, but he's still critical.
The first twenty four hours are crucial, and then the twenty four after that.

He meanwhile, is having the strangest dreams. A chimney comes into them,
and a vent to an underground bunker. A round globular light: a full moon
or else the sun as it lowers itself into the horizon, followed by blackness.

Sometimes there's a floundering yellow balloon that keeps drifting away
Sometimes he thinks he hears the high whine of a drill. Now and again
what might be voices fade into the distance.

Two balls of string back he was certain he could hear his wife talking.
He doesn't know what's she's doing here? She's never been interested
in scuba diving or giant turtles. His breath bubbles through the snorkeler

and there's a dull thudding going on inside his head. He's back in Farna
where Moriarty the fat slob has him in a headlock and won't let him go,
and there's a sharp pain in his groin where he's kicked him for his troubles.

And then, a jelly-like euphoria spreads slowly, creeping along the inside
of his limbs as the morphine soothes him once more. Now his dreams
are of laburnum, purple wisteria, clematis in full flower

and of a stiff breeze buffeting the tall grass in the field above the house
until it turns into a great green swell below the rocks north of the Mizen.
Three Castles Head, he thinks: I'll maybe try to come ashore here.

When they take the ventilator off the consultant explains. 'We've had to cut a hole in your cranium, four inches by four. We've placed the shell in the cavity under your intestinal sac to keep it alive.

We'll leave it for six months then we'll re-structure it back on. In the meantime be careful how you bang your head!'

Electrical Engineer

He's all wired up, chest, arms, legs, the wires connected to the monitors. Rural electrification is the phrase that comes to him. The West of Ireland, 1956. People gathering in the parish hall to hear about the scheme, him selling it to them, answering their questions. Supposing a child shoved a nail in a socket? What about the farmer over in England, all his cattle electrocuted in the byre? Electricity is much safer than a mowing machine or even a motor car, he says.

Would the wires attract lightning, cause a hay-shed to burn down? Hay sheds caught fire before electricity was ever heard of. Fellows talking afterwards in the pub, saying they'd not let it in the house. It would put an end to the scoriorting and the card playing, and the faeries.

But the women are all for it. Imagine being able to get up and boil the kettle without having to put down a fire first. An electric iron would be great ease, and no more milking by the light of a lantern, or cutting turnips in the pulper and feeding the cows by the smell of their breath, or falling over the dog. 'Out here all you see is the dark and the stars and the dull glow over the town five miles away.'

But the lorries carrying the telegraph poles are too wide for the country roads, and the wheels sink in the bog holes, and it's he has to bear the brunt of it, with farmers telling him the poles can't be stood in the middle of a field, because the bull would horn them and they'd be a lot safer over by the ditch. Him trying to get them into a straight line and avoid sag on the wires.

And the glory in the end, of seeing them stretching away in the distance, mile after mile, all the way to Black Sod Bay and Ackill Sound. Next thing every half-baked electrician west of the

Shannon, fellows who barely knew the workings of a screwdriver jumping on the bandwagon.

Thirty bob a light and thirty bob a plug, and people trying to skimp by having as few sockets and as few plugs as possible, a light in the hallway, in the kitchen, the parlour, one up on the landing. 'the shadow of it will do for the bedrooms, there's no need for plugs up there, who'd ever want to boil a kettle upstairs!'

Things loosened out after a while. Those who took it the first time around said they wouldn't be without it now. Next thing it all took off. People wanted an electric this and an electric that. Stuff for wedding presents: electric blankets, bedside lamps, hot plates, irons, Sacred Heart lamps, radios, record players -you could listen to the likes of Pat Boone singing April Love, or Slim Whitman yodelling any time you like.

He went freelance when all his peers were heading for Boston and the motorways of England, supplying suppliers in all of the Western Counties. 'Cable was where the big money was,' he says, 'Mayo was a spread out county.'

His feet are blue with the cold. There must be water after getting into his wellingtons. The nurse covers them and makes him comfortable. Now he's remembering their courting, and the guy who played the saxophone at the dance hall in Ballina. The warmth of the blanket spreads upward and his face breaks into a wide smile.

The cardiac arrest was an electrical failure, and the stroke followed, but there's no serious damage. It's nothing that can't be fixed. His fourteen grandchildren were here to visit him on Sunday. Now a fine boned well-dressed woman walks in. 'Just like I told you,' he says, 'I always did well in Mayo.'

The Hurler

His fingers are cupped to catch the sliotar in flight.
The marks of the hurley still decorate his knuckles.
'How are you today, Tommy?' 'Great, thank God.'
'Would you walk down the corridor there for me.'
As he gets into his stride he straightens himself up.

He can hear the Artane Boys Band ahead of him,
Any minute now he'll take his place at left wing back.
Any minute now the Bishop will throw in the ball.
Tommy will be waiting for the high ones, make sure
he gets to them first, or if not God help whoever does.

The All Ireland medals are great, but nothing touches
the heat of battle, the scent of victory, the fear of defeat.
Last year in the Munster Final he held Christy Ring
to a single point. He was man of the match, ahead of
Liam Devanney, Pat Stakelum, and John Doyle.

The memories are what matter to him now.
They've seen him through some tight corners.
'You're walking straight as an arrow Tommy,
you can go on home as soon as you're ready.'
There'll be bonfires in Toomevara tonight.

Joe

'Will you try a little exercise for me Joe?'
'Yes.'
'Can you tell me your name?'
'Yes.'
'What's your name?'
'Yes.'

'Joe! Joe! Are you with me Joe?'
'Yes.'
'Do you know what this is?'
'Yes.'
'Can you tell me what it is?'
'Yes.'

'It's a knife, can you say knife?'
'Yes.'
'And what is this?'
'Yes.'
'It's a glass Joe. Can you say glass for me?'
'Glass.'

'What's that you have there, Joe?'
'Yes.'
'Can you tell me what that is?'
'Yes.'
'It's a rosary beads Joe.'
'Yes.'

'Would you say a little prayer for me Joe?
'Yes.'
'Our Father!'
'Yes.'

'Who art in heaven!'

*Hallowedbethynamethykingdomcomethywillbedone
onearthasitisinheavengiveusthisdayourdailybread
andforgiveusourtrespassesasweforgivethose
whotrespassagainstusandleadusnotinto
temptationbutdeliverusfromevilamen.'*

Snagged

No matter how often he pulls on the cord
the lawnmower won't kick. It's like that old banger
he had one time. Or the bike he went to school on, the chain
coming off on every steep hill, the pedals going round in a fresh-air spin.
He'd be last into school, all blackened with grease.

It comes back to him these nights in dreams
where something announces itself then refuses to start.
Sometimes it's the banger, sometimes a composite,
a marvel: half lawnmower, half banger, half bike.

At primary school his hand was always the first up.
Adds and take-aways, tables, multiply and divide.
The Master said, the quickest he'd ever taught.
Even now, the figures are all lined up in his head

but the words get snagged on the way to his throat.
'Relax,' she says, 'can you point out the pictures
on the pad? Bucket: yes. Spade: right. Sand castle:
excellent. Which doesn't belong? The bed, good.'

Learning to Dance

Six long months I spent up in Dublin,
Six long months doing nothing at all,
Six long months I spent up in Dublin,
Learning to dance for Lanigan's Ball.

Wash:	Face, good man.
Read:	Book, good man yourself.
Bake:	Cake, you're flying it now.
Knife:	Cut, excellent, very good.
	You can practise this at home with the Missus.

Yesterday we looked at some pictures, remember.
Can you point out the cup and the burger. Good.
Now can you show me the jug and the pencil. Fine.
The boat and the jug! You've got one of them right.
This time the toaster and the tomatoes. Look again.
Very good. Pencil and tomato. Right. Yes. Good.

She stepped out and I stepped in again,
I stepped out and she stepped in again,
She stepped out and I stepped in again,
Learning new steps for Lanigan's Ball.

O.K Martin, let's go on to the next level.
I'll point out a word, and this time, let's see
how many matching words you can come up with.

Wash:	Hands. Face. Cake! I don't think
	you'd wash a cake? Cup. That's better.
Eat:	Bread, yes. Jam, yes. Cake, good.
	Excellent. You've got the hang of it.
Sleep:	Bed, yes. Cot, good. Table! It would be
	uncomfortable trying to sleep on a table.
	Something softer: sofa, good man yourself.

She stepped out and I stepped in again,
I stepped out and she stepped in again,
She stepped out and I stepped in again,
Learning new steps for Lanigan's Ball.

Her Father's Daughter

She's at the bedside holding his hand when the doctor comes.
His broad-boned muscular frame is propped up with pillows.
Her face mirrors his in shape and smile, her hair is raven dark
as his was once. He's making a good recovery, she can see that.
Speech, posture, the movement on his left side, have all improved.

Whatever they've been saying to each other in Romany, as well as
his cheerfulness, has cheered her up. He'll be home soon she thinks.
The doctor, going through the battery of tests confirms this, except,
he explains, 'the part of the brain that projects images on to the retina
has been damaged, and although there is nothing wrong with his eyes

per se, the chances of fully recovering his field of vision are slim.'
He doesn't understand the doctor's language, but his daughter does.
He can't see the weather-change on her face, but he knows the taste
of bad news, and when she touches him again he feels the heartbreak.
She knows he'll take this very hard. He knows something bothers her.

The grief reflected back echoes and multiplies. They've always
tried to hide such from each other. It never worked. As the first
drops trickle and curve along her chin, his face mists up, until
his matching held-back tears tumble out. She dabs them with
her fingertips, then wipes her own with the back of her hand.

The Day Room

Sean sits alone with the telly on, but there's nothing interests him.
Not long since he'd have been right there in Attenborough's world:
Elephants on safari, Bullfrogs in Borneo, nocturnal secrets of Bengal Tigers.
Or Patrick Moore with his eighty eight Constellations, Spiral Galaxies,
Andromeda, Gemini, and the four quarters of the Zodiac.

In the ward the two nurses are making up the bed. They've honed
their skill to the rhythm of a dance. One billows the sheet, the other
catches it. They spread it out like the ocean, let it fall, then smooth
the air pockets, tuck the ends under the mattress. All in their stride
as they chatter and sometimes laugh.

They lay the counterpane across, fold it back, turn the corner down.
Lastly they frump the pillows, puff them up, and it's done. When Sean
comes back he won't know any of this, but he'll feel it in his bones,
the smooth sheets, the lightness of touch, coming to him in his sleep,
all the way from Kerala and Mindanao.

The Golfer

Portmarnock Golf Links was where this love affair took off.
Watching Joe Carr, amateur, as a boy, following him as he played
against the world's best: Jack Nicklaus, Arnold Palmer, Sam Snead.
His own game never reached anywhere near,

but it became his life. There were the pure moments:
hitting the perfect drive, or finding the heart of the green,
or the thrill of sinking an outrageous putt. All those times
he played as well as he ever could.

Dogged in combat, magnanimous in victory, gracious
in defeat. A gentleman to the last but no quarter given.
Five down with five to play he still wouldn't give in,
defeat unthinkable to the end.

Lazarus they called him. Again and again he came back
from the dead, coming out of the bunker however deep.
Four times in this last year he's been down, and out.
Each time he pulled through, getting back on course.

Last week, delighting in his youngest granddaughter
he lifted her onto his shoulders and shouted: 'Fore.'
This time, so far into the rough it couldn't last.
Out in Portmarnock the flags are at half mast.

Tom Brogan

We were on our way back in the mini-bus, after a wedding
in Ballinasloe. Traffic was heavy, Jimmy Dineen was driving.
Someone had started a sing-song. I remembered an appointment
I was likely to miss. I'd look out for a phone box in Athlone Town.

'Pull in there Jimmy,' says I, when we came to the Shannon bridge,
but I couldn't hear myself with the noise. So I went to give him a tap
on the shoulder, only to find my hand was asleep. Malone on my left
gave me a funny look, asked was I alright. I never felt better in my life.

Next thing I heard him telling Dineen to pull in. When I heard the word
Ambulance, I thought one of the lads in the back must have taken a turn.
'I have a phone call to make,' I said, but the words didn't come out.
Only then did it dawn on me, it was me all the fuss was about.

Next day in the hospital in Mullingar my voice came back. I never
recovered the use of my right arm or leg. It doesn't bother me too much,
but it's a puzzle how something like that can happen, and the only one
doesn't realise, is yourself. I felt a bit of a Gom, to tell you the truth.

The Grief

Ronnie is upbeat. It's what he does best. Whenever
the team loses he'll be the first to say: 'Look lads,
we'll be back next year, stronger than ever.'

The same when his wife walked out. 'You don't get it,' she said.
He hadn't a clue what it was he didn't get. In no time he was down
the pub telling good-ones about wives walking out on their husbands.

Fierce craic altogether fair play to him, you'd nearly have to laugh.
No one knew what he really felt, about anything. He didn't know.
He wouldn't let himself. And there he is now, with his lopsided

smile, jollying up the nursing staff and the cleaners. The consultant,
who has seen it all before says: 'Give him a couple of days. The grief
of it hasn't hit him yet.' It took a week, but when the dam burst
                              there was no stopping.

The tears of a lifetime. And what he's remembering is the morning
after he turned eleven, his mother giving him a slap across the face
for calling his sister a thief. Later on, above in the hay-shed

he sobbed his eyes out, then gritted his teeth. 'They'll never see
me crying again.' Which they didn't, until this.

Peter

'O.K Peter, We'll have another go.
Lean forward. Look out over your toes.
Now look down, and up,
good man yourself. And again.
Show me how you'll do it at home.

Before you stand up
rock forward, look down,
stick your bottom out,
lift, and up.
That's better.

We'll give it one more go?
That's much better than yesterday.
Was it easier?'
'*No.*'
'You just need a drop of oil to get you going.

Are you ready to try out a bit of a walk?
Big step forward.   Big step backward.
Big step to the left.   Big step to the right.
And turn around.   Great, much better.
Do that on your Zimmer when you get home?'

Willie Nelson

A selection of locks and keys, door handles and bolts,
taps and plugs, are lined up on the large wooden board;
along with a row of hooks, switches, dials and buttons;
a kettle, toaster, and a full array of kitchen appliances.

A child of the 60's. The headband with the hair clamped
at the top and stretching down as far as his belt fans out
across the whole of his lower back. His fingers splayed
to take on the challenges ahead. He begins with the Yale.

The key doesn't fit the lock at first, but he's determined.
It takes him a couple of tries to get the chain-lock in place.
'You've got to keep the burglars on their toes. They're not
going to skip your place just because you're incapacitated.'

Next he pushes a plug into its socket, switches it on, and off,
unplugs it again, and repeats the exercise half a dozen times.
'Try ringing the door-bell with your index finger. Well done.
Move the bolt over and back. Do it again. Click, clack. Good.

Can you pick the cane off the floor? Open your fingers. Grip.
Now see how you go on with pouring the drinks.' He takes
the jug of water and pours it into a set of coloured glasses.
One topples and lands on the floor. Just as well it's plastic.

And all the time I watch his wild wiry grey jungle
and think Willie Nelson. The scraggy half cut beard,
the laughing eyes. I expect to see him walking on-stage
tuning his beat-up guitar, and singing as good as ever.

Little things I should-a-said-n-done, I just never took the time.
You were always on my mind. You were always on my mind.
Later I see him in the canteen with his wife, sipping coffee.
It will soon be time to catch their bus back to Ballyfermot.

Maeve

I'd been in an induced coma for more than a month.
When they brought me round I had locked-in syndrome.
The only bit of me I could move was my right eyebrow.
Every inch of my body ached, but my head was the worst.
The morphine gave some relief but it made me hallucinate.

There was this talking candle, with a hole burnt for the mouth.
There was a sand dune I tried to prevent myself sliding down
but my fingers couldn't get a grip. I could see its endless slope
and knew if I let go I'd never be heard of again. Then there were
three old crones perched on a roof beam, cackling and laughing.

'We have her where we want her now,' they gloated. It was them
made me determined to get better. 'You've surprised us all Maeve,'
the consultant said. 'We didn't think you'd make it. We never thought
you'd come this far.' 'Thanks Doctor,' I said, 'you've all been good to me.'
It had been six weeks before my speech came back, albeit only in whispers.

'It's all down to you,' he told me. 'There's a fair amount of physical damage
but no cognitive impairment. You're doing really well, don't push too hard.'
The one thing I couldn't do was open my eyes. A young student from Trinity
came up with a solution. A pair of wire springs on the inside of my glasses.
A firm of opticians developed the patent. The chief exec came to fit them.

The trial lasted ten seconds. Soon as I blinked my eyelids closed again.
Everyone was deflated. The chief exec talked about minor adjustments.
But I knew it was a non-starter, and to tell the truth I wasn't too bothered.
Now, my sense of smell can pick things up a mile off. Alcohol hand gel,
the nurses perfume. I can smell the porridge coming three wards away.

And you wouldn't believe my hearing. Noise filters in, contracting pipes,
trollies delivering supplies. I listen to early morning sounds as the hospital
awakes. I hear folk greet each other, or not. I can separate out their footwear,

the click clack of high heels, the shuffle of slippers, the squeak of trainers, the solid intent of male leather soles, the quickstep of the female flat shoe.

Sometimes I'll hear the hushed hurry of a trolley pass during the night, some poor person being rushed off to emergency. Or I'll hear the nurses whispering when everyone's asleep. They were on about me once, how brave I am, and how gentle and determined. How I appreciate little things. With a lump in my throat I'll admit it's the truth. It wasn't always the case.

I listen to my iPod. Handel's Messiah, Luke Kelly, and Leonard Cohen. Or Richard Burton, reciting Dylan Thomas and Gerard Manley Hopkins. Sometimes I imagine I hear voices as from a far off railway station, and though I grieve for my former life I'm never down. The catastrophe has taught me gratitude. These days I seem to be living out of my better self.

The Hokey Kokey

You put your left leg in, you put your left leg out.
In out, in out, shake it all about.
You do the hokey kokey and you turn about.
That's what it's all about.

O.K. Bring your left leg forward.
And up. Brilliant. Perfect, try to hold it there.
Now catch the grip, pull yourself towards it.
And again.   Good.

Now straighten your right leg.   Good,
Where did you say you grew up?
Keep the leg straight if you can.
Now lift yourself up.

We'll done.   And again.
Now turn to your right.   Good.
And to your left.   Good.
And again.   Good.

Bring your left leg out again
As if you were getting into bed.
Now pull yourself up.   We'll done.
Steady there on your own.   We'll done.

Now lie back again.
One leg in.   Now the other
And lift.   Move it in if you can.
Now the other one.   Excellent.

Now, to get back out again.
First the right.   Good.
Now the left. That's a bit hard, o.k.
Now, see if you can lift your head.

Hold your balance.
Hold it.   Lovely.
That's what it's all about.
Getting into bed and out.

Gleann Na Smol

Sitting her up on the saddle until she's comfortable
he straps her feet into the stirrups, and sets the dial.
'Fifteen minutes,' he says, 'Bohernabreena and back.
Don't worry about getting tired, the gears will kick in
automatically.' So off she sets at a nice pace, her legs
revolving with the pedals. As she gets into her stride
it all starts to come back: her taking the lead going up
– she had strong legs then, him in front on the way down,
rounding the corners at a slant, leaning in to the wind.

After ice creams at Bohernabreena they'd head on
for Gleann Na Smol. They'd stop near St Anne's,
hide their bikes under a furze bush inside the ditch,
and walk down to the old Cemetery. Sometimes,
if the path was muddy, she enjoyed the squelch
as the mud sucked at their boots, and she liked
the way the sheep eyed them, confirming them
as a couple. It was a grand place for courting.
It was here, above the reservoir he proposed to her.

Afterwards, going through the wrought iron gates
they reviewed the two-hundred-year-old headstones.
'In memory of Brigadier Henry Doyle 1773-1812,'
– the Napoleonic wars no doubt – 'and his beloved wife
Jennifer 1785-1867.' That was a long time to be alone.
They hoped that nothing would ever set them apart,
– in sickness and in health – well into the 21st century.
Then they climbed carefully down to the water's edge
and walked all the way around the reservoir.

A low sun sparkled the cover of snow on the mountains.
The valley turned golden, like the great bowl of the world,
and over the water, an orchestra of silence. They lingered

as long as they could, it was dark when they reached home.
She waited for almost a week before telling her parents.
They returned each year, with the kids when they were
big enough for bikes, and alone after they'd grown up.
The years had challenged them both. 'My Warrior Queen,'
he calls her. She knows he hasn't faced up to this one yet.

'Nice one Maeve. A personal best, Bohernabreena and back
in fifteen minutes. Are you sure you went all the way?'
'Gleann Na Smol,' she smiles, 'we went all the way.'
He unstraps her feet, helps her into the wheel chair.

Stroker

He sits on the chair between the window and the bed.
Double chin, beer belly, tattoos decorating both arms.
'I'm doing alright Doctor. The weekend out was nice.'
'Did you stick to the instructions?' 'I tried very hard.'
'What about the beer and cigs?' 'I won't lie to you.
I did as good as I could.' 'And how good was that?'
'A few pints, just catching up with the fellas like.
A couple of fags. I didn't go wild or anything.'

'Well, it's not for me to tell you how to carry on.
What I will tell you is you got off light this time.
Next time you might not be so lucky. Life style
is an issue here, you're high risk for another one.'
'I hear what you're saying Doctor, and fair enough.'
Later he ruminates aloud: 'I'm a working class man
but it makes no odds, I could be Arthur Guinness.
In here we're all the same. We're all strokers.'

Cognitive Test

'Can you tell me what year it is?'
'I don't even try to find out.'
'What season?'
'Autumn.'
'The month?'
'February/March.'
'What day is it?'
'Would Tuesday do?'
'What date?'
'I don't care about dates.'

'What country are we in?'
'Republic of Ireland.'
'What city?'
'Dublin.'
'Which district are we in?'
'Would it be Templeogue?'
'What floor are we on?'
'I'd say the top floor.'

'How's your writing?'
'It's been better.'
'What are you like at spelling?'
'I'm a good speller.'
'Can you spell 'world' backwards?'
'Not at the moment.'

'How old are you?'
'It's hard to tell.'
'How are you feeling?'
'I can't answer straight away.'

'Can you say: no, if, and, or but?'
'No ifs or buts.'

Mr Brennan

'Where were you born, Mr Brennan?'
'I forget.'

'You were born in England. What year were you born?'
'I don't know.'

'Nineteen Twenty One. Do you know that makes you over ninety?'
'O my God.'

'What year is it now?'
'O God, it's gone. I was, oh it's gone.'

'It's Two Thousand and Twelve.'
'I knew all that one time. I know nothing now.'

'How's your breathing?'
'Not too good.'

'I'm going to check your pulse. How are you with the walking?'
'Poor.'

'I'll have a listen to your heart. Give me a big breath. And out. Good man. What year did you get married Mr Brennan?'

'O God almighty, I think was it maybe, was it Nineteen Twenty Two.'

Stan

'I played football for Home Farm as a schoolboy.
I got a trial for Bolton Wanderers but didn't go.
I used to play for Shamrock Rovers later on.
I was fast; a bronze medal in the Olympics.

Who was the best player I saw in my time?
George Best is the one that stands out.
He had wonderful skill in his body.
I was good, but not that good.'

'I'll see you again in six months.'

Recipes

Mammy and Daddy were always afraid of the glimmer man.
He'd come round to your house to check if your cooker was warm.
You'd be fined if you were caught using it when you weren't supposed to.

There was no fruit to be got, apart from the home grown apples
and you couldn't get hold of them unless you had an orchard yourself
or you were living in the country. My younger sister spent the whole war

Wondering what an orange tasted like. I'd try to explain to her
it tasted orangy, but that only made her cross. What class of a taste
is orangy, she'd ask, and so it went, round and round, a-ring-a-ring-a-rosy.

In the end to shut her up I said it was a class of a yellow taste.
She asked me did I mean like stirabout? I said no, not like stirabout,
it was a different class of yellow altogether. That satisfied her well enough.

One evening we came home from school and my mother said:
there's some lovely sandwiches for yiz. They tasted like bananas.
Where in the name of God did you get bananas and there a war on says I?

Did you like them says she? They're gorgeous altogether says I
but where did you buy them? Ate them she says, and don't be talking.
It's parsnips you're after having she tells us later, with banana flavouring.
They were nicer than bananas if you ask me. I wish we had those recipes today.

Jacko

'Were you a heavy drinker?'
'No. I was a binge drinker.'

'You've the cut of a man who
knows how to stand at a bar.'

'You asked me so I told you.
That's how it was back then.

I worked seven days a week,
double shift, sixteen hour day.

The Boars Head, Caple Street.
Ten or twelve pints of a night.

I tried the non-alcohol stuff.
The sugar didn't suit me.

It was a long time ago.
I've been dry for years.

I get bad headaches now
and regular dizzy spells.

I don't sleep very well.
I put it down to stress.'

'Are you depressed?'
'You could say that.'

'I'll arrange a brain scan.'
'You'll have to find it first.'

Preventative Medicine

'And what about exercise?'

I've brought the exercise bike in from the shed.
This time of year I'd be only making excuses.
I can watch telly while I'm doing my stints.'

'You're carrying too much weight.'

It's the tablets you prescribed.
Two weeks in, my legs started to swell.
So I stopped taking them.'

'Your drink patterns?'

I don't drink all the time
but when I'm on it, I'm on it.'

'It would help if you gave that up rather than the tablets.
The tablets are not the problem. The problem is your liver.
Your liver is beginning to pack up.'

                              'Oh' ...

'Stay away from alcohol. Double up on the bike.
Go back on those tablets. See you in six weeks.'

Home Visit

I was sitting in my Parker Knoll when I saw him
coming past the hedge and looking in the window.
It was him alright. He had only been dead a year.
I got a bit of a fright but I was glad to see him again.
The second time he appeared I asked him to come in.

But he never answered. Four evenings in a row he
stood outside, vaguely lonesome, looking past me.
Then one evening while I sat there waiting to see him
a troupe of Polish dancers in brightly coloured frocks
came through the door and stood over by the dresser.

Yellows and reds and purples, with short silk stockings
and buckled shoes, they were half the height of the table.
I took a quick glance at the clock and when I looked back
they were gone. They kept coming for about three weeks.
Then at the same time one evening the gargoyles appeared.

A whole gang of them, biting and tearing at each other
and no sound coming out of them. I could see their jaws
wide open, and their green teeth, and their eyes bloodshot
and their gullets bloody like they were after eating raw meat.
I was badly shaken. I had to say something to my daughter.

'I saw your father again yesterday evening,' I said to her,
'wearing that old trousers and a new hat.' I didn't mention
dancers or gargoyles, and I should have kept my mouth shut
because the very next day Doctor Collins arrived at the door
with his brown leather bag and a stethoscope round his neck.

'How are you doing Mrs O'Brien?' he says. 'Fine,' says I.
We chatted away for a good spell. He asked who knitted
my cardigan, and where I came upon my nice blue slippers?
I could see him taking everything in. Then he started asking
which day of the week it was, and what month of the year

and who was the president of Ireland? 'Michael D Higgins.'
I told him. 'And where does he live?' 'Above in the Áras'
says I, 'sure where else would he live.' Then he asked me
which programmes I liked watching on telly. I told him
the television was banjaxed, the pictures were all blurred.

I said I preferred the radio. I've no trouble at all seeing
what's on the radio. 'There's not much wrong with you
Mrs O'Brien,' he says, 'and you haven't got dementia.
You've got something called Charles Bonnet Syndrome.
It's nothing at all that a decent pair of glasses won't fix.'

I haven't seen my husband, or the dancers, or gargoyles
for months now, and the television has improved no end.
I miss seeing himself, and I miss the little dancers in their
finery and silk stockings. I take off my glasses evenings
in case they decide to show up. I've had no luck so far.

Mr and Mrs Goodwell

'How am I doing is it? I'm doing fine.
It's the Missus wanted me to come.
She's a nervous class of a woman.'

'What's bothering her?'
'She's on about seizures, but it's all in her head.'
'Why do you say that?'
'Do you think if I had a seizure I wouldn't know it?'

'Do you have any abnormal incidents or dizzy spells?'
'I'm a bit forgetful now and again but that's about it.'
'Will we bring herself in so?

❋

Hello Mrs Goodwell, and how are you doing?'
'It's not me. It's him. He won't face up to it.'
'What won't he face up to?'
'The seizures.'

'I had a seizure nine years ago.'
'He had two in the last month.'
'I did not.'
'And one the month before that.'
'I told you, I don't HAVE seizures.'
'Do you see what I mean Doctor?'

'What are the symptoms Mrs Goodwell?'
'It's in his sleep, he goes all rigid like.
He starts to make these gurgling noises,
teeth gnashing like a broken dish-washer,
talking gibberish and frothing at the mouth
like he's having some kind of an epileptic fit.'

'How often has this happened in the last six months?'
'Four times that I know of, but I'm not bound to wake up.'

'There's nothing wrong with me. It's all in your head.'
'It's all in YOUR head.'

The Mother

She'll go for a few days or even a week, and she's fine.
Then of a sudden she'll take a bad notion and turn on me.
She won't know me, or she'll think I'm her grandmother.

When I go to work she starts hiding things all over the place.
The other week I found coins stuck in the butter, and a fifty
folded into a narrow crack between the door jam and the wall.

She's afraid of being burgled. She locks the doors
then hides the keys thinking that will keep them out.
The keys turn up in the strangest places. The other night

I couldn't get her to eat supper, her mouth was clamped shut.
Later I saw her spitting into her fist. When she went to bed
I found her key hidden in the drawer

She's got a lot worse since we saw you last.
Out in the garden during the warm weather she kept saying
'I've never liked Lanzarote. I didn't want to come.'

Samuel

For a while there he thought he was one of their sons.
He'd say: 'how are you doing Martin?' Or: 'have you
been talking to John lately, when is he coming home?'
And then he thought he was someone letting on to be
one of them. 'Stop trying to take me for a fool.'

For a while after that he thought he was a burglar.
That's when the hullabaloo started in earnest,
shouting and roaring and waving a stick, and
ordering himself out or he'd send for the guards,
and making her wait at the gate for the squad car.

One evening she heard a fierce banging overhead.
The next thing, he came running down, head first
into the back of the closet, – she hadn't seen him run
like that for years, wonder he didn't break his neck –
and whimper: 'there's two burglars in the bathroom.'

After she had quietened him down, she went up
and found a big split in the mirror. He spent
the rest of that week cowering in a corner.
He said they were trying to rob him. He began
to hide money in his socks and underwear.

When the paranoia sets in he'll shout at the mirror:
'who are you?' and tell himself to get out of the house.
On a good day he'll spend hours looking down the valley.
He'll say to her something like: 'did you ring the Mammy?'
Or: 'if I had the money I'd whiten this place with sheep.'

Kevin Street

I grew up in Kevin Street. Did I tell you that?
Close to Guinness's Brewery. My father worked
at Guinness's. Everybody in Kevin Street worked
at Guinness's, if they worked at all. The nuns prepared
us for First Communion. We learned our Catechism:
Who made the World? God made the world.
The nuns gave us silver mints to practise with.
I always liked the taste of the silver mints,
Holy Communion was never as nice after.
I wore a blue suit and short trousers.
Everybody in our street worked at Guinness's.
if they worked at all. Kevin Street, did I tell you?

The coopers were held in the very highest regard.
If somebody was a cooper there was no more to be said.
It was handed down from father to son. They didn't use
tape or measure, it was all gauged with the naked eye.
The oak was left to season for two years, then prepared
and steamed to get the right curve on the stave, so that
they'd lock into each other. They burned wood shavings
to char the insides and seal the wood. Then the metal hoops.
Thirty two gallons to the barrel. The coopers were held
in the highest regard. The nuns gave us silver mints.
Holy Communion after the mints was never as nice.
Did I tell you I grew up in Kevin Street.

Jennifer

She's walking up and down the dayroom when I come in.
Her nails are manicured and polished, her lipstick bright red.
Over her fine cheek bones her hair is washed and combed and
sits high on her head. Her eyes are ablaze, and the leather strap
of her bag is poised on her shoulder, as a declaration of intent.

'It's a complete waste of time, this,' she tells me. 'I could be
at home helping my brother run the business. It's too much
for my parents now. I only signed up for the qualifications
but the whole thing's a shambles.

I know I shouldn't grumble but it's a disgrace, never mind the cost.
Anyway, I've told them I've had enough. I'm leaving and that's it.
I'm just waiting for the taxi now. The way things are around here
I expect the taxi will be late as well.

But I shouldn't be taking it out on you.' 'That's no bother,' I say.
'It does no harm to have a good moan. Otherwise are you o.k?'
'I'm fine,' she says. We talk about the nice autumn weather then,
how the virginia creepers turn from purple to russet. As I get up
to leave, she says: 'you will come again next week, won't you?'

Train Driver

He boards the train wearing a cassock. The white lace of his surplice
smudges on the grease of the cab door. The signals are changing
from Latin to Greek but it makes no odds, he's top of the class in both.
First, a student for the Priesthood, then a lay missionary in Biafra.

Here on his bedside locker a bottle of Lucozade, a box of grapes
unopened. He's saving them for the level crossing before Mullingar.
The nurse butters his toast. Would he like marmalade? He says yes,
but he'd rather have the Kola nuts and that nice thick Egusi soup.

The train rounds a wide sweep between Ballygar and Galway. Its smooth
incessant *Kyrie eleison, Kyrie eleison,* repeats itself *in saecula saeculorum.*
Coming to a red signal he puts the brakes on squeal. The couplings
link the decades on his rosary beads, the joyful mysteries,

the sorrowful mysteries, the whine of the makeshift ambulance bringing in
the wounded, trucks carrying sacks of meal out-manoeuvring the blockade.
He remembers, before the war broke out, the sticky heat, beautiful women
in their bright coloured dresses, the sins of his youth a long-closed book.

Passing under the viaduct he takes off his biretta, bows low. He'll be back
at Maynooth for Vespers. He blows on the charcoal, puts it in the thurible.
He stands inside the Altar-rails in his shiny black shoes, his train-driver's cap.
The Deacon adds incense, and smoke wafts up to the stained-glass windows.

The sweet tang of burning incense mingles with the odour of the dead.
Starving children stare out at him pleading, can't they see how helpless he is?
The train waits in a siding, the rails following the endless circle of his rosary.
Soon he'll be on his way: Portarlington to Port Harcourt, Enugu to Athenry.

Lori

She doesn't suffer fools, or anyone.
Staff come in numbers to give her a bed bath
Or a change of clothing. You can hear her
Two corridors away. *'Get away. I said No. NO.'*

I approach her with respect, and some trepidation.
'What do YOU want?' She asks. 'Nothing,' I say.
'Is it money you're after?' 'I'm not after money.'
'It's just as well, because you won't get any here.'

Next time I hold my peace. Her eyes are closed
But her radar picks me up. *'What do YOU want?'*
I continue to remain silent. *'You want to learn
To talk you,'* she says. *'That's what YOU want.'*

At the Nurses Station

'At the cross her station keeping ... '
From: *Stabat Mater,* Jacopone da Todi 1236-1306

The brown cardboard folders are loaded onto the trolley
where they lie at a slant; these track records of infirmity.
When the consultant and his entourage arrive: – registrar,
junior doctor, a pair of medical students from Trinity –
he gets a verbal update on temperatures, restlessness,
episodes during the night. He scrutinises the notes
from his previous visits, then each patient receives
his undivided attention. Afterwards further notes
are added, and medication reviewed.

Finally there's the scrutiny of the brain scan.
On the monitor he traces the hemispheres with his finger,
points to the dark edges where the haemorrhage occurred.
Over his shoulder you watch as vague hallucinatory forms
take shape, like figures conjured from moving clouds:
a hang-glider, a dog with big ears, a barn owl at night.
Or the winged headgear of an old style French nun.
Or: *the Holy Ghost over the bent /World broods*
with warm breast and with ah! bright wings.

As he drew near to Jericho, a blind man was sitting by the roadside begging; and hearing a multitude going by, he inquired what this meant. They told him, "Jesus of Nazareth is passing by."

And he cried, "Jesus, Son of David, have mercy on me!" And those who were in front rebuked him, telling him to be silent; but he cried out all the more, "Son of David, have mercy on me!"

Luke 18: 35-39

The Gardener

'Squeeze my hand,' the Doctor says. Which is, more or less,
what Jesus says to the blind man at Jericho, as told in Luke
and depicted by the artist Anna Duncan in the hospital chapel.
The man sits under a palm tree close to the water's edge
with his begging bowl on his lap. Three stern bearded men
tell him to shut up but he doesn't. He cries out, loud as he can:
'Jesus, Son of David, have mercy on me.'

Mercy is not the Doctor's immediate concern, he's checking
to see if the patient's grip has come back, and the patient is not
a beggar, he's a gardener beyond in Ballymun. His handshake
– the shovel-size hands with calluses as thick as a sandwich –
used to be like a jockey's. Firm and probing, with that look
that takes in the measure of another, nails down the character
of man or horse. He tries to squeeze, watches the doctor's face.

He was digging a tree root over in Mrs O'Donoghue's garden
when this thing came over him. First a numbness on his tongue
as if he was after having a tooth out. Then the spade taking leave
of itself, and next thing looking at the sky through the branches
of a pear tree, as if they were only trying to tell him something,
with his right hand gone blind. Jesus touches the beggar asking:
'What do you want?' He answers: 'Lord, that I may see again.'

Now there was a woman who had been suffering from haemorrhages for twelve years; and though she had spent all she had on physicians, no one could cure her.

She came up behind him and touched the fringe of his clothes, and immediately her haemorrhage stopped. Then Jesus asked, "Who touched me?"

When the woman saw that she could not remain hidden, she came trembling; and falling down before him, she declared in the presence of all the people why she had touched him, and how she had been immediately healed. He said to her, "Daughter, your faith has made you well; go in peace."

Luke 8: 43-48

Monica

'Would you like a cup of tea,' is always her first remark.
It's a long time since she's revelled in lavishing hospitality:
the family parties, big dinners, birthdays. Stuffed pork steak
was a speciality. But that's all gone now, along with everything.

The fall was inevitable, everybody said. Out in the yard
at the back of the care home. She thought she was
collecting tinder to start the fire. They found her
lying in a heap, with her pelvis fractured.

Today her son has come to visit. He intends to take her out
but the rain has started, so they do the internal tour instead.
Down the long corridor to the entrance and the coffee shop,
turn left, past the stairs to the children's ward, to the Chapel.

Lunchtime Mass is starting. She remembers the responses:
Lord have mercy. Christ have mercy. Lord have mercy.
After Communion she falls asleep. When she wakes
her son wheels her over to the healing stations.

He shows her the one with the woman who had an issue
of blood that had bothered her for twelve years. As Jesus
walks through the jostling crowd she touches the fringe
of his cloak, and he feels the power go out from him.

He's looking over his left shoulder to see who touched him.
The woman, barefoot, is down on one knee in the wet street.
Monica's eyes are filled with tears. 'You're a lovely man,'
she says to her son. 'Would you like a cup of tea.'

Just then there came a man named Jairus, a leader of the synagogue. He fell at Jesus' feet and begged him to come to his house, for he had an only daughter, about twelve years old, who was dying.

When he came to the house, he did not allow anyone to enter with him, except Peter, John, and James, and the child's father and mother. He said, "Do not weep; for she is not dead but sleeping." He took her by the hand and called out, "Child, get up!" Her spirit returned, and she got up at once.

Luke 8: 41-42, 51-52, 55-56.

A Prayer

Today, a young woman comes with the straggled gait
of a person off a long-haul flight. She's wearing jeans
and un-zipped calf length boots, and, like someone
who hasn't since childhood, kneels before the altar.

Beyond her shoulder the twelve year old daughter
of Jairus is being raised to life. The disciples wait
discreetly by the door. Jesus takes her by the hand.
The girl, thin, with stringy hair, is resting on her arm,
her parents transfixed, their only child restored to them.

As King David, in sackcloth, once begged that his son,
the child of his adultery with Bathsheba might be spared,
the young woman's awkwardness is eased by desperation.
As she turns to leave her face is streaked with grief.
I believe Lord, help thou my unbelief.

They arrived at the country of the Gerasenes. As he stepped out on land, a man of the city who had demons met him.

Jesus asked him, "What is your name?" He said, "Legion"; for many demons had entered him. They begged him not to order them to go back into the abyss.

Now on the hillside a large herd of swine was feeding; and the demons begged Jesus to let them enter these. So he gave them permission. Then the demons came out of the man and entered the swine, and the herd rushed down the steep bank into the lake and was drowned.

Luke 8: 26-27, 30-33

The Celtic Tiger and the Gerasene Demoniac

It wasn't just the Gerasene demoniac. The whole country was possessed.
We thought we were on the Tiger's back, but it turns out he was on ours.
Going from mixing concrete to meeting with Planners at The Shelbourne
was mad enough, then we got into the re-zoning and the brown envelopes.

The Rolex, and the Saville Row suits, and silk shirts flown in from Paris.
The Bentley, and the Gulfstream Jet, and the Mansion out on Killiney Hill.
We were drunk on the adrenalin of it. When the whole thing went belly up
we were well bolloxed. The Banks, then NAMA wanting their money back.

Tracking my affairs was easy. The Penthouse Suite in Lower Manhattan,
and the debacle in Dubai. And here I am now in my top of the range
4X4 wheelchair, down in the chapel, watching that poor demoniac
as Jesus raises him up, and the pigs with the devils in them rush for the cliffs.

I'm not much of a religious man but I like a good story. The last of my pigs
went over the cliff this morning. I told them about my account in the Caymans.
'The devil is in the detail,' they said. But the devils are in the pigs, I know that
                                                                          now.
The whole time, right up to the night I collapsed I hadn't felt right with myself.

Not just the extravagance, but the shaping and the shammery that went with it.
And now, with my movement at less than ten percent and my speech scrambled,
I feel better than I have done for years. All that madness is gone, over the cliff
along with the pigs. We're free men at last, myself and the ex-demoniac.

Once, when he was in one of the cities, there was a man covered with leprosy. When he saw Jesus, he bowed with his face to the ground and begged him, "Lord, if you choose, you can make me clean."

Then Jesus stretched out his hand, touched him, and said, "I do choose. Be made clean." Immediately the leprosy left him.

Luke 5: 12-13

Diogenes and the Leper

The barrel this Diogenes lived in was a small flat over in Terenure.
A plumber by trade, and good at it too, but something came over him
when he hit forty. He took time off from work and never went back.

Sunday Mass became claustrophobic so he went into St Patrick's
when it was empty, sat in its cul-de-sacs and caverns. He hated
getting on a bus, hated going into town, so that stopped too, as did

going down to the Mountain Dew on a Friday night. Instead he'd walk
the Canal banks or out along the Dodder. He wouldn't answer the door.
Whenever his sisters called he put the run on them. The flat was

waist deep in soup cans and filth. It didn't smell good, neither did he.
What brought it all to a head was falling down the stairs. It was as if
someone had pushed him. He lay there for days. In the end a neighbour

called the Guards. They broke down the door. The clothes had to be
cut from him at the hospital. When the nurse pulled off his socks
his toenails were seven inches long, green with dirt, and twisted

like a set of corkscrews. His blood was as thin as water.
But he had only been concussed and there was no long-term damage.
He fitted in to the ward very well, started to mix, the fear had left him.

When he saw the station with the leper cleansed, it reminded him of
himself. The warning bell dropped, and the bandages drifting away,
people no longer peeping at him from doorways. When they told him

the name of the syndrome and who it was called after, he only laughed.
'Does that make me a philosopher?' They told him that it did.
His sisters sorted the flat. The smile stayed on his face till the day he left.

The Horseman

To this day nothing beats being out on the gallops first thing,
cold air around his ears, the sounds of snorts and hoof-beats
and the sun coming up; except, going to the winners enclosure
after momentum has slowed to a walk and the horse turns back.

It's not just the applause, but the satisfaction for its own sake.
It's been a long time, but that old rush of blood still happens
regularly in his head. He sits in the care home in silk pyjamas.
The walls of his small room are decorated with the glory days

he thinks are still here; when he measured himself against the best,
getting the leg up on every race-track in the land, Newmarket,
Epsom, York. 'The best brain in the weighing room,' they said,
the day he out-piggotted Piggott in the Coronation Cup.

Then the training years, the winners over jumps and on the flat.
The Gimcrack, Cesarewitch, Fighting Fifth. What he misses now
is the healthy smell of horse manure, pungent as a Cuban cigar;
the adrenalin rush of race day, the feel of the reins in his hands.

Life goes at a canter most days, but there are times he forgets
when he's off the bridle with fear, his mouth held in a grimace
his elbows taut. At ninety one he's close to the winning post
but a life's habit, he doesn't want to make his run too soon.

The Good Tears

A small seizure has brought him here from the plains of Meath.
Now that small seizure has become the big C. It has opened him
to his history and his life. He remembers as a child hearing about
Brinsley McNamara and the Valley of the Squinting Windows.

He remembers the beatings as a boy, from the Christian Brothers
and the life-long love of literature they gave him. He's read Dante
and Descartes, Thomas Aquinas, Duns Scotus, Beckett and Yeats.
He's read Ulysses several times but never finished Finnegans Wake.

He's pleased to see that Kavanagh was a patient here, and Behan,
though mercifully not at the same time. And Oliver St. John Gogarty
who doctored here, – Stately, plump Buck Mulligan – as Joyce has him,
and Swift who stabled his horse while Gulliver went on his travels.

He's been writing stories set in forties Meath. I mention my day job.
He says he hasn't been near a church for years. A broken marriage
and other regrets, but there remains a resonance with Godly things.
'I've cried across the broken bones, and the blessings of my life

these last two weeks,' he says with another burst of full-on tears.
I tell him how St. Ignatius Loyola believed that the clearest sign
of gratitude is uncontrollable crying. 'Good tears,' he calls them.
'Like Heaney's turf cutters. Going down for the good tears.'

CPSIA information can be obtained at www.ICGtesting.com
Printed in the USA
LVOW11s1533020915

452547LV00002B/429/P